What makes a Car go ?

Sophy Tahta

Designed by Lindy Dark
Illustrated by Stuart Trotter
Consultant: Derek Sansom
Cover design by Russell Punter
Cover illustration by Christyan Fox
With thanks to Sarah Cronin

KT-170-416

CONTENTS

Parts of a car

Cars are made up of many different parts which all work together to make the car go. You can see some of these parts here and find out how they work later in the book.

Fuel is stored in a fuel tank beneath the car. The driver takes off this lid to fill up the tank at a garage.

The car body is made from strong, metal panels.

An exhaust pipe under the car carries burned gases away from the engine.

The car's battery stores electricity to work the lights and other parts.

Engine

The engine burns fuel to run the car. The engine is usually in the front of the car.

Pictures with the symbol ☐ can be downloaded from www.usborne-quicklinks.com

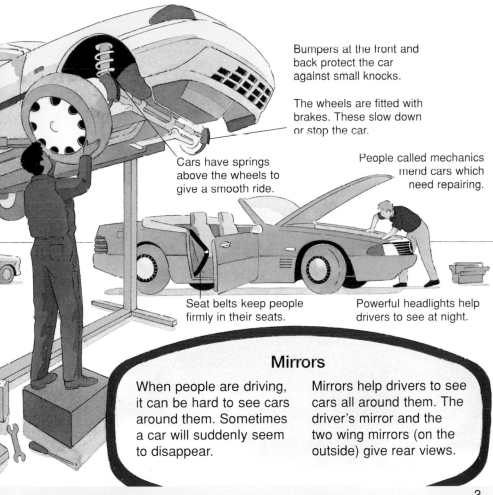

Bumpers at the front and back protect the car against small knocks.

The wheels are fitted with brakes. These slow down or stop the car.

Cars have springs above the wheels to give a smooth ride.

People called mechanics mend cars which need repairing.

Seat belts keep people firmly in their seats.

Powerful headlights help drivers to see at night.

Mirrors

When people are driving, it can be hard to see cars around them. Sometimes a car will suddenly seem to disappear.

Mirrors help drivers to see cars all around them. The driver's mirror and the two wing mirrors (on the outside) give rear views.

Internet link Go to *www.usborne-quicklinks.com* for a link to a website where you can design your own car online - then test-drive it!

Inside the engine

Cars need energy to go. The engine produces energy. It does this by burning fuel and air inside tubes called cylinders. Here you can see how this energy turns the wheels.

6. The axle turns the back wheels which push the car along.

1. The fuel is lit by an electric spark from a spark plug.

2. The burning fuel forces drums, called pistons, to move up and down inside the cylinders.

3. The moving pistons turn a rod called a crankshaft.

5. The drive shaft makes this rod called an axle go round.

4. The crankshaft turns this rod called the drive shaft.

Cut-away of engine

Gear box

Spark plug

Cylinder

Piston

Crankshaft

Different drives

Power from the engine can go to the back wheels, the front wheels or to all four wheels. Whichever system a car uses, is called its drive.

Cars with four-wheel drive have extra grip.

4

How a piston works

Each piston does four movements, or strokes, as it goes up and down twice. Pistons move quickly in turn to keep the crankshaft spinning all the time.

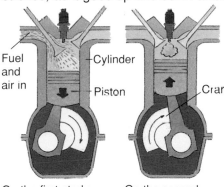

Fuel and air in — Cylinder — Piston

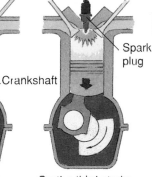

Crankshaft — Spark plug

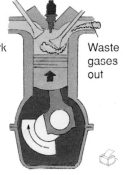

Waste gases out

On the first stroke, the piston moves down. It sucks fuel and air into the cylinder.

On the second stroke, the piston goes up. It pushes the fuel to the top of the cylinder.

On the third stroke, the fuel is lit by the spark plug. The explosion forces the piston down.

On the fourth stroke, the piston moves back up. It pushes waste gases out into the exhaust pipe.

Piston power

When a car is going along at 80km (50 miles) an hour, a piston in the engine may move up and down about 2,500 times each minute.

Try counting roughly how many times you can tap a pencil on a table in one minute, and then imagine how fast a piston moves.

Internet links Go to **www.usborne-quicklinks.com** for links to websites where you can watch animations that show how an engine works.

Fuel and energy

Some of a car's energy is used to turn the wheels and some of it is used to make electricity.

Internet link Go to **www.usborne-quicklinks.com** for a link to a website where you can find out how cars get their fuel with a clickable diagram.

Electricity is stored in the battery. It runs parts such as the lights and horn and also lights up the dashboard.

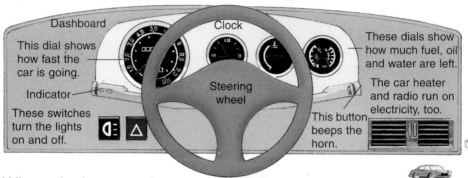

Dashboard

Clock

This dial shows how fast the car is going.

Indicator

These switches turn the lights on and off.

Steering wheel

These dials show how much fuel, oil and water are left.

The car heater and radio run on electricity, too.

This button beeps the horn.

Where fuel comes from

Fuel for cars is made from oil. Oil is found under the ground or the bottom of the sea. It was formed millions of years ago from the rotten remains of tiny sea animals.

People use giant drills to find oil and pump it up.

Drill   Oil

6

All lit up

Drivers use lights to see at night and to let other cars know what they are doing. See if you can tell which lights cars are using next time you are out.

Two red brake lights come on at the back of the car when the driver presses the brake pedal. Most new cars also have a third brake light in the middle of the rear windscreen.

Using energy

Cars burn fuel to make energy, just as you eat food to keep you going. The more energy cars use, the more fuel they burn.

Big, heavy cars and trucks use more fuel than smaller ones.

Cars burn more fuel to go fast or uphill.

An uphill climb

Cars use more energy when they go uphill because they are driving against gravity. Gravity is a force which pulls everything down.

Cars need more energy to go uphill as the force of gravity pulls them back.

Gravity makes it easier for cars, and you, to go downhill.

Cars use headlights and red rear lights to see and be seen in the dark.

Orange lights flash on each corner when the car has problems. These are called hazard lights.

A single orange light, called an indicator, flashes at the front and back when the car turns left or right.

Gears and steering

Gears make cars go at different speeds. Most cars have four or five gears to go forward and one gear to make them go back.

Cars start off in first gear. This gives extra force to move the wheels.

Second and third gears help cars to pick up speed and climb uphill.

What are gears?

Car gears are tiny, toothed wheels in the gear box. They make the drive shaft turn at different speeds.

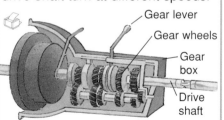

Gear lever

Gear wheels

Gear box

Drive shaft

In some cars, the gears change on their own. In other cars, the driver moves a gear lever to choose which gear will turn the drive shaft.

Did you know?

In 1930, a Model A Ford car drove 5375 km (3340 miles) in reverse gear, from New York to Los Angeles in the USA. It drove back to New York in reverse gear, too.

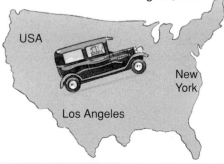

USA

New York

Los Angeles

Internet link Go to *www.usborne-quicklinks.com* for a link to a website where you can take an interactive look at gears and other simple machines found around the home.

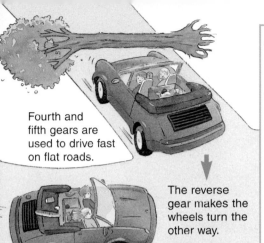

Fourth and fifth gears are used to drive fast on flat roads.

The reverse gear makes the wheels turn the other way.

Steering a car

The steering wheel is joined to the front wheels. The driver turns the steering wheel to point the wheels the correct way.

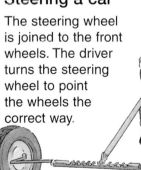

A smooth ride

Springs and shock absorbers help cars drive smoothly on bumpy roads. They are called the car's suspension.

Shock absorbers are tubes of gas which stop the springs from bouncing too much.

Spring

This anti-rolling bar stops the car from tipping over around corners.

Shock absorber

A rough ride

Early cars had bad suspension and thin wheels. They bumped up and down a lot and were not at all comfortable to ride in.

Slowing down

The driver presses the brake pedal to slow down or stop the car. Here you can see how it works.

The brake pedal pushes oil along pipes to the wheels.

The oil pushes brake pads against a metal disc in the wheels to stop the wheels from turning.

Brake pads

Oil

Brake pedal

Disc

Friction

Brakes use a force called friction to work. Some forces make things start or stop. Friction tries to stop things from moving when they rub together.

Brake lever

Brake pads

You can see how friction works on a bike. Press the brake lever and see how the brake pads rub against the wheel.

Friction between the brakes and wheel stops the wheel from spinning.

Friction between your shoe and the road also helps you to stop.

Friction between the brake pads and wheel wears the pads down. When they are very worn they need to be changed.

Internet link Go to **www.usborne-quicklinks.com** for a link to a website where you can try an online friction experiment using wind-up toys.

Getting a grip

Wheels have grooves called tread. Tread helps wheels to grip the road when the car brakes or turns. It is like the tread on your shoes, which gives you better grip, too.

The pattern of tread helps to push water away on wet roads.

Chains can be hooked onto wheels to grip snowy roads.

Racing cars do not use tread on dry tracks. They only use tread when it rains.

Friction in the air

There is also friction between moving things and air. Air pushes against moving things to slow them down. This sort of friction is called drag.

Cars have rounded smooth shapes which move through the air more easily. These are called streamlined shapes.

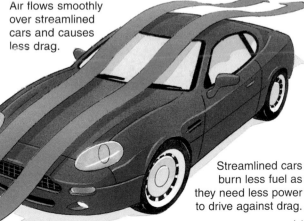

Air flows smoothly over streamlined cars and causes less drag.

Streamlined cars burn less fuel as they need less power to drive against drag.

Making a car

Internet link Go to **www.usborne-quicklinks.com** for a link to a website where you can watch animations of a car being made on an assembly line.

Millions of cars are made each year in car factories all over the world. Each car is made from thousands of parts.

Here you can see how a car is put together, step by step, on a moving track called an assembly line.

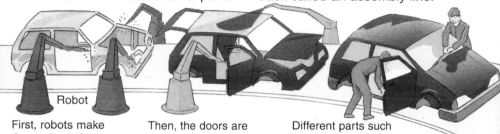

First, robots make the car body from sheets of metal.

Then, the doors are put on and the car is sprayed with paint.

Different parts such as the windows and lights are fitted next.

Crash testing

Every few years, car makers design a new model of car. They crash it to test how safe it is and then look at the damage to see how it can be made safer.

Some cars have air bags. These inflate in a crash to protect people in front.

The front and back of the car are made to take the shock of the crash and crumple.

Seat belts hold people in place.

Crash dummies show what happens to people in a crash.

This strong, metal cage protects people inside.

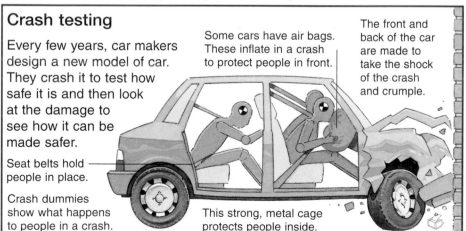

12

Spot the badge

Car makers have their own badges. Try and find out who these badges belong to and see if you can spot them on any cars. Check your answers on page 23.

1
2
3
4
5
6
7
8

Engine

Now the car body is joined to the engine and the controls are added.

The seats are put in later and the wheels go on at the end.

13

Cars and pollution

Cars send out waste gases called fumes from their exhaust pipes. These are unhealthy to breathe and cause dirt, or pollution, in the air.

Heat-up

A layer of gases called the atmosphere surrounds the Earth. It traps the Sun's heat like glass in a greenhouse. Extra car fumes in the atmosphere trap more heat. This is known as global warming.

Deadly lead

Lead is often added to fuel to make older engines run better. Lead makes exhaust fumes harmful to breathe. All new cars now have to use fuel without lead.

Clean-up

A filter called a catalytic converter can be put on car exhausts. It cleans some of the fumes, but not others.

Some heat escapes into space.

Heat trapped by greenhouse gases

Greenhouse gases

Global warming melts icy areas. This could cause seas to flood the land.

Waste gases can turn rain sour, or acidic. Acid rain poisons trees and lakes.

Global warming could make parts of the world dry up.

Smog is made when car fumes mix with sunlight. It hangs over cities on hot days.

New kinds of fuel

Car fumes are caused by burning fuel. The oil that makes car fuel will one day run out. People are looking for cleaner ways to run cars which use less oil.

Electric cars

Electric cars run on batteries. They make no pollution, but soon run out of power. People are trying to make better ones.

Sun-powered cars

A few cars use energy from the Sun. They have special panels which change sunlight into electricity, but they are not powerful enough to use everyday yet.

Fuel from plants

Fuel can be made from plants such as sugar cane. It causes less pollution and will not run out.

Sugar cane is grown to make fuel in Brazil.

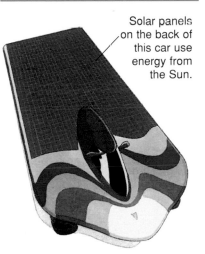

Solar panels on the back of this car use energy from the Sun.

Internet link Go to **www.usborne-quicklinks.com** for a link to a website where there is lots of interesting information about global warming.

Cars and traffic

Cars can cause traffic jams, as well as pollution. Here are some ways that people can cut down on traffic and pollution.

Internet link Go to *www.usborne-quicklinks.com* for a link to a website that challenges you to find the fastest way to travel across a town in the year 2024.

In some towns it is easier and cheaper to use trains and buses. Trains carry hundreds of people who might otherwise go by car.

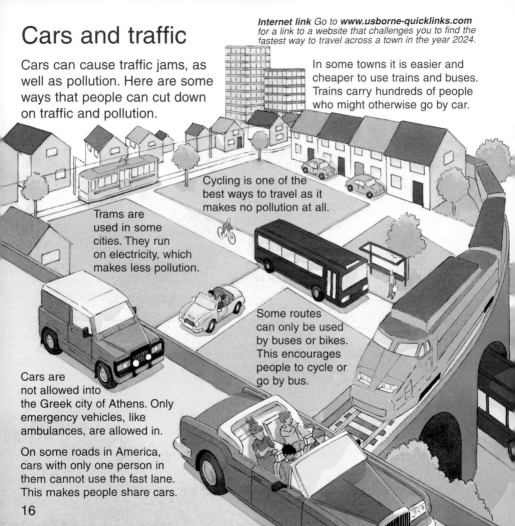

Cycling is one of the best ways to travel as it makes no pollution at all.

Trams are used in some cities. They run on electricity, which makes less pollution.

Some routes can only be used by buses or bikes. This encourages people to cycle or go by bus.

Cars are not allowed into the Greek city of Athens. Only emergency vehicles, like ambulances, are allowed in.

On some roads in America, cars with only one person in them cannot use the fast lane. This makes people share cars.

16

Did you know?

There are over 650 million cars and trucks in the world today.

If they were all parked in a long line, they would go around the world about 65 times.

Bumper to bumper

In 1980, a traffic jam stretched north for 176 km (109 miles) from the south coast of France. It was the longest ever recorded.

Paris

France

Driving with computers

Computers are now used in some cars to avoid accidents and traffic jams. Car makers have already tested the ideas below.

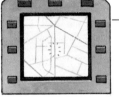

Some cars have a computer screen on the dashboard. It shows the driver which roads to take to avoid accidents.

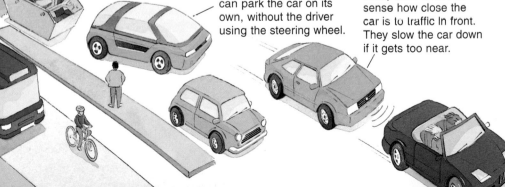

A computer in this car can park the car on its own, without the driver using the steering wheel.

Computers in this car sense how close the car is to traffic in front. They slow the car down if it gets too near.

Cars in the past

The first cars were made over 100 years ago. They were slow and unreliable to begin with, but people soon learned how to make them faster and better.

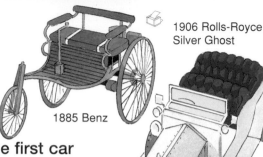

1906 Rolls-Royce Silver Ghost

1885 Benz

The first car

The first car to be sold to the public was made by Karl Benz in Germany in 1885.

"Best car in the world"

Many early cars were very grand. The Rolls-Royce Silver Ghost was called "the best car in the world" because it was so splendid to drive.

The first assembly line

In 1913, an American named Henry Ford built the first assembly line to make cars cheaply and quickly. This meant more people could buy them.

Over 16 million Model T Ford cars were made between 1908 and 1927.

Internet link Go to **www.usborne-quicklinks.com** for a link to a website where you can find out more about Henry Ford and the Model T.

Cars for everyone

All kinds of cars were made in the 1920s and 1930s, from racy sports cars and luxury cars to big, family cars.

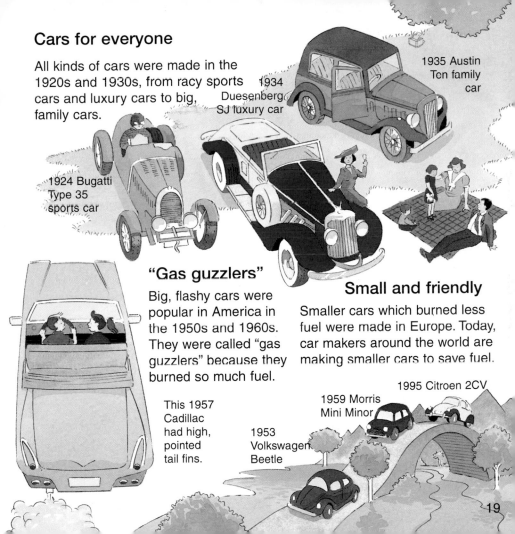

1934 Duesenberg SJ luxury car

1935 Austin Ten family car

1924 Bugatti Type 35 sports car

"Gas guzzlers"

Big, flashy cars were popular in America in the 1950s and 1960s. They were called "gas guzzlers" because they burned so much fuel.

Small and friendly

Smaller cars which burned less fuel were made in Europe. Today, car makers around the world are making smaller cars to save fuel.

This 1957 Cadillac had high, pointed tail fins.

1953 Volkswagen Beetle

1959 Morris Mini Minor

1995 Citroen 2CV

Racing cars

Racing cars have much more powerful engines than ordinary cars and go a lot faster. Different kinds of racing cars drive on different tracks.

The car body is light and streamlined to cut through the air.

Back wing

Formula One cars

Formula One cars take part in Grand Prix races. Grand Prix means big prize in French. Drivers win points for their finishing place in each race. The driver with the most points in the year is the World Champion.

Formula One cars race many times around a long, twisting track. Each time around is called a lap.

Wings at the front and back help to keep the car on the ground. Air rushing over them presses the car down.

Racing drivers wear a crash helmet and fireproof clothes for protection.

Front wing

Brake duct

Powerful brakes can slow the car down in seconds. Air blows through brake ducts to cool them down.

Formula One cars can go over 380 km (240 miles) an hour.

Internet link Go to **www.usborne-quicklinks.com** for a link to a website where you can take an interactive tour of a Formula One racing car.

Dragsters

Dragsters race each other in pairs down a short, straight track. The whole race only lasts about six seconds.

Dragsters can drive at up to 480 km (300 miles) an hour.

Parachutes slow down dragsters at the end of a drag race.

Rally cars

Rally cars take part in races called rallies over mountain, country and desert tracks. Rallies are split into stages. The driver who finishes all of the stages in the best overall time wins.

These extra lights are for driving in the dark.

Rally cars have extra strong suspension to drive over bumpy ground.

A co-driver next to the driver reads the map and gives directions.

21

Unusual cars

All these cars are unusual in different ways. Some are built to do special things and others are made to look as amazing as possible.

Orange car

This orange car was built in the 1970s by a fruit company. The company used it as an advertisement.

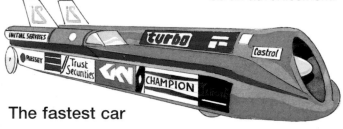

This is Thrust 2. It broke the land speed record in 1983.

The fastest car

A car called Thrust SSC broke the land speed record in 1997 when it sped across the Nevada Desert in America at 1228 km (763 miles) an hour.

On the Moon

This electric moon buggy was the first car in space. Astronauts drove it on the Moon in 1971 and left it there when they returned.

The moon buggy helped the astronauts to explore where they had landed.

Internet links

For links to more websites with information about cars, go to the Usborne Quicklinks Website at **www.usborne-quicklinks.com** and click on the number of the website you want to visit.

Website 1 – Discover more about the history of cars, cars found around the world, and cars that have appeared in films, including James Bond cars and the Batmobile.

Website 2 – Find out about the different parts of a car, with clickable diagrams.

Website 3 – Take a virtual tour of a Mercedes-Benz museum, test-drive a racing car or build your own car online.

Website 4 – Find out how different parts of a car work by watching animated diagrams.

Website 5 – Explore an interactive racing car, with animated diagrams, fascinating facts and photo galleries, and find out about the science, design and dangers of today's racing cars.

Website 6 – Learn about the science of speed in an online exhibit, with stories and games.

For links to all these sites go to Usborne Quicklinks at www.usborne-quicklinks.com

---

Answers to page 13

1. Peugeot
2. Honda
3. Cadillac
4. Porsche
5. Alfa Romeo
6. Mitsubishi
7. Volkswagen
8. Bentley

Index

First published in 2002 by Usborne Publishing Ltd., Usborne House, 83-85 Saffron Hill, London EC1N 8RT, England.
www.usborne.com Copyright © 2002, 1993 Usborne Publishing Ltd. The name Usborne and the device ♀ ⊕ are Trade Marks of Usborne Publishing Ltd. All rights reserved. No part of this publication may be reproduced, stored in a retrieval system, or transmitted in any form or by any means, electronic, mechanical, photocopying, recording, or otherwise, without the prior permission of the publisher. Printed in China.